BIRTH AFFIRMATIONS FOR LABOR

TO VIEW MY FULL RANGE OF BOOKS SIMPLY SEARCH FOR

REMI HICKS ON AMAZON

HOW BIRTHING AFFIRMATIONS HELP WITH CHILDBIRTH

Affirmations help to promote a feeling of calm and confidence during labor. This is extremely important because of the way your mindset alters your hormonal state.

The hormones released during your labor dictate how you feel, how fast or slow your labor progresses, how safely your child will be delivered, and much more.

GOOD HORMONES:

Oxytocin is very important during labor. Also known as the "love hormone", it is produced during intercourse, after ovulation, during labor, delivery, and breast feeding. It elicits feelings of nurture and love.

Endorphins are a type of neurotransmitter that have a relaxing and pain-relieving effect. Endorphin levels rise steadily as labor progresses and pain increases in unmedicated labors.

BAD HORMONES:

Adrenaline is frequently referred to as the "fight or flight" hormone. Stress, fear, and intense pain cause the release of adrenaline. If a woman has these emotions during labor, she may create too much adrenaline, slowing down the process.

Low oxytocin levels during labor and delivery can cause complications by making labor take longer by causing contractions to halt or slow. This can promote extra bleeding after the baby is born.

Low endorphin levels will cause you to experience more pain than necessary. This may then lead to you feeling more need to opt for higher levels of chemical pain relief which can then lead on to other interventions.

WHAT'S THE SOLUTION?

The good news is that you can help your body produce more oxytocin and endorphins by simply maintaining a calm, relaxed, and self-assured mindset!

This is why affirmations are so useful during childbirth. Not only do they help you to maintain a happy, positive mindset throughout the entire process, they also act as a distraction which can really help to stop overthinking which may cause adrenaline levels to rise.

We have broken down the affirmations in this book into sections so that you can quickly navigate to the stage of labor you are in and find relevant affirmations when you need them.

We hope you find this book useful and wish you and your baby all the happiness in the world!

TIPS FOR USING AFFIRMATIONS EFFECTIVELY

The first tip I would give is to read through the affirmations and find the ones that really click with you at the time. You don't need to use them all, you may even just find one affirmation that particularly resonates with you and use that for the majority of your labour. This is because everyone has different concerns that some affirmations will address better than others.

If you find that the affirmation you are using is losing its effectiveness then you can quickly refer back to this book and find a new one! You may even find an affirmation that you didn't like very much before, but in the heat of the moment or as your situation and emotions develop, you may find that it will begin to appeal to you and really help you at the time.

Remember to repeat the affirmation and really believe it. Affirmations aren't something that you hope will happen, they are a statement of truth in the present. So focus on the words as you repeat them and truly believe them.

We have printed this book with single sided pages so that you can remove any affirmations that you particularly like. This enables you to use them as affirmation cards or hang them on a wall or refrigerator for example as a reminder to do your affirmations!

We hope this helps and now we will move right on to the affirmations that I have chosen especially for this book…

BIRTH AFFIRMATIONS FOR EARLY LABOR

THIS IS THE
DAY I'VE BEEN
WAITING FOR

I LOOK
FORWARD TO
THIS EXPERIENCE

MY MIND IS
RELAXED.
MY BODY IS
RELAXED.

I AM PREPARED.
I AM READY.

I AM SAFE.
MY BABY IS
SAFE.

EACH CONTRACTION IS BRINGING ME CLOSER TO MEETING MY BABY

MY BODY
KNOWS JUST
WHAT TO DO AND
I TRUST IT

I ACCEPT AND WELCOME LABOR

I AM RELAXED
AND HAPPY THAT
MY BABY IS
FINALLY COMING

BIRTH AFFIRMATIONS FOR ACTIVE LABOR

I AM
SURROUNDED BY
LOVE AND SO IS
MY BABY

BIRTH IS POWERFUL. I WILL LET IT EMPOWER ME.

I RELAX
AND MY BABY
RELAXES
WITH ME

WOMEN ALL
OVER THE WORLD
ARE BIRTHING
WITH ME RIGHT
NOW

I AM
STRONGER
THAN I EVER
IMAGINED

MY BODY IS
CAPABLE AND
STRONG

WITH EACH DEEP BREATH, I FEEL BETTER AND BETTER

MY BODY WAS DESIGNED TO DO THIS

BIRTH IS THE ULTIMATE ACT OF LOVE

I FEEL CONFIDENT
I FEEL SAFE
I FEEL SECURE

I BREATHE
DEEPLY AND I
AM CALM

I TRUST MY
BODY TO KNOW
WHAT TO DO

BIRTH AFFIRMATIONS FOR DEALING WITH PAIN

WHEN I FEEL I
CANNOT DO IT,
I KNOW I AM
CLOSE

MY CONTRACTIONS CAN NEVER BE STRONGER THAN ME BECAUSE THEY ARE ME

PAIN IS A
PART
OF THE
PROCESS

I WELCOME SURGES.
I DON'T FIGHT AGAINST THEM.

PAIN IS
POWER. PAIN IS
PROGRESS.

SHE BELIEVED
SHE COULD AND
SO SHE DID

WITH EVERY CONTRACTION I AM CLOSER TO BRINGING NEW LIFE TO THIS WORLD

BIRTH AFFIRMATIONS FOR THE FINAL PUSH

I AM READY TO
GIVE BIRTH TO
MY BABY

I AM FIERCE
YET FLEXIBLE

I AM READY TO MEET MY BABY

BIRTH AFFIRMATIONS FOR IF YOUR PLANS CHANGE

I MAKE THIS CHOICE OUT OF LOVE FOR MY BABY

I AM STRONG
ENOUGH TO LET
MY BABY BE
BORN THE WAY
MY BABY NEEDS

OUR START DOES
NOT DETERMINE
OUR FUTURE

MY BABY
GIVES ME THE
STRENGTH TO DO
ANYTHING

MY BABY
TRUSTS ME AND
I TRUST THIS
PROCESS

Printed in Great Britain
by Amazon

44689157R00056